PLOWMAN'S EARTH

WILLIAM MUNDELL

PLOWMAN'S EARTH

THE STEPHEN GREENE PRESS
BRATTLEBORO, VERMONT

ACKNOWLEDGMENTS

Grateful acknowledgment is made to the following publications for permission to reprint poems that appeared originally in their pages: *The Atlantic Monthly* for "Passing Remark," copyright © 1956, by The Atlantic Monthly Company, Boston, Massachusetts; *American Forests* for "After Logging," "An Old Tree Falls," and "When Spring Is Early"; The Middlebury College *Saxonian* for "Reminiscence"; *The New York Quarterly* for "Genesis," reprinted by permission from *The New York Quarterly*, no. 13 (Winter 1973); *The New York Times* for "Now Are the Hills on Fire," © 1954 by The New York Times Company, reprinted by permission; *The Providence Sunday Journal* for "Return"; *Yankee* for "Horse Story," reprinted with permission from the December 1940 issue of Yankee Magazine, published by Yankee, Inc., Dublin, N. H.

This book has been produced
in the United States of America:
designed by R. L. Dothard Associates,
composed by Vermont Printing Company,
printed and bound by Murray Printing Company.
It is published by the Stephen Greene Press,
Brattleboro, Vermont 05301.

Library of Congress Catalog Card Number: 72-91796
International Standard Book Number: 0-8289-0183-x

For Miriam

and John Andrews

CONTENTS

WILLIAM MUNDELL

THE poetry of William Daniel Mundell requires no introduction to his fellow Vermonters, to readers of *Poetry* or *Poet Lore*, or to owners of his first book of poems, *Hill Journey*, published in 1970 and sold out within months of its appearance. All of these know Mundell as a sensitive observer, a polished craftsman, a master of several forms and styles of poetry—all of them his own. Perhaps all that a friend can contribute to an appreciation of the poems in this, his second book, is a note on the quality and range of the poet's experience, a background rare in any age and certainly exceptional in an era of specialized working and living like our own.

Mundell is a poet with deep roots in his local place—a narrow upland valley in the southwest corner of the Town of Newfane in southeastern Vermont. He was born in his own house, Brookside, and, with few interruptions, has spent his life there, with the swift waters of Hunter's Brook at his front doorstep and the steep hills from which it falls in his back yard. Like some of his favorites— Burns, Emily Dickinson, and Dylan Thomas—he is a poet who knows so well his physical and social surroundings that he can write about them always freshly or take them for granted as he transcends them. Because he is a hill-country native of the oldest stock, who can tell dryly witty tales about long-dead village characters in an impeccable Old Vermont accent, it is tempting to present Mundell as a character in his own right. To do so would be to slight the qualities of his sensibility and the technical mastery of his craft which reflect a lifetime of study and practice.

William Mundell wrote his first poem on the living room hearth at Brookside when he was seven years old, a doggerel ballad celebrating the then recent discovery of the tomb of the Pharaoh Tutankhamen. He has been writing in the same room ever since, at a desk crowded with books of poetry and criticism and manuscript drafts of his own work (like Yeats, he is a multiple reviser). While he has studied at two colleges and can quote readily the critical dicta of modern masters like Pound and Eliot, he is largely self-educated. He attributes his precision of language to fine old-fashioned teaching in the ancestral one-room schoolhouse, but his feel for the rhythms and flavors of poetry has developed from his own reading, evidenced by the ease with which he can recite from memory lines of such classics as Spenser and Shakespeare. When he talks quietly about the making of poems to a few friends or to a class at the Cooper Hill Writers Conference, he can be as deceptively homely and self-deprecatory in his language as any village artisan explaining the fundamentals of his craft. This simplicity of language in his criticism, as in his poems, is the mark of the expert workman.

Fine workmanship is the key to Mundell's art, as it has been the guiding principle of a life rich in interests and varied in occupations. He is a professional carpenter and road-builder, a skilled stonemason (self-taught), a designer-builder of ski trails and residential developments. He has, at different times in his life, supervised a local WPA program, run his own contracting business, served as a radar technician and completed officer training in the U.S. Marine Corps during World War II, built and run his own ski area and captained his own ski patrol, and achieved the highest efficiency rating of the State of Vermont during a fifteen-year career as a Highway Maintenance Foreman. He has held several town offices, from Justice of the Peace to Selectman. He is an expert skier, hunter, and naturalist, an educated amateur mineralogist, a prize-winning photographer. Full-page color photographs of woodland scenes around Newfane have provided a visual accompaniment to several of Mundell's poems published in *American Forests,* the magazine of the American Forestry Association. At the Brattleboro Camera Club, where he is one of the judges, the poet is best known for his color transparencies of the fern and flower designs traced by the frost on winter windows. He is also Assistant Editor of *Poet Lore* and a member of the Poetry Society of America. In 1968 he won the Stephen Vincent Benét Narrative Poetry Award.

MY SOLITUDE IS MOUNTAIN

My solitude is mountain
beyond the valley of the day's concern,
beyond the river of the crowd's voice,
farther than the last trickles of laughter,
higher than the flora of friends' love
and the fauna of strangers' wishes,
where only the insistent winds of longing
touch my ledges of loneness.

Yet there are those high wings
above me aspiring
in a blue more lonely.

BEFORE YOU GO

(FOR MY FATHER)

Before you go where other suns
raise Eden lush from golden seeds
and weave it round you as a robe,
walk once more on our barren hill;
oh walk with me our field of weeds.
Our scythes made fire on the stones;
our wheels laid thunder on the road.
Oh lift once more that starry load
that, building, bent us toward the ground.

Before you go where other suns
attend the garden of your dream,
remember here where shadows meld
there was that music of the stream;
some sunshine touched our stubble field.

ANOTHER GARDEN

Did you see flame
dying in October leaves?
Did you wake to frost;
lie down in plenty,
arise in want?

Where now can we gaze
on green wild-growing?

Asters have moved to stars.
The moon is one pumpkin.
Shall we furrow the sky's loam,
tap its misty seas,
toil in a stubborn soil
studded with stone
of constellations?

Shall we knock our hoes
against Orion and the Pleiades?

THE GRAVEL PIT

Among these sea-mouthed pebbles of spent tides
agates stare like ancient serpents' eyes.
My pick strikes cautiously that ocean's floor
and darkness slithers back from probing light.

Here time reveals its sacred calendar:
the years of sand, the centuries of clay.
I break earth's chalice and I rob time's grave
as men who loose the atom from its tomb.

We meant to brighten earth, to lift the night,
but wind and tide will write their own report.
What sloughing reptile thing will rise to learn
that man laid all his treasures down in dust?

LATE FARMING

Through years and every season's need
your hands, now mine,
still callous on the plow,
broadcast the seed.

All days are one.
It was today we reaped and gathered in
except the days are years;
the barn looms dark and empty
and the chores are done.

All days run backward
toward the night.
I follow and each day
I cross your days
and spend the quick remaining light.

AN OLD TREE FALLS

An old tree falls
not in a night, creaking and calm,
while ants sleep under its curling bark
and squirrels lie in its furling leaves;
not in the soft alarm of dawn
when birds call and drum
the morning on its hollow limbs.

An old tree falls at the time
of the whirlwind of its remembrances,
after the night has written its name
in lightning upon the scroll of the sky
and spoken its praise in sentences of thunder.

An old tree falls at the time
of the celebration of the winds,
when there is argument in the weather
and indecision in the seasons.

An old tree goes to rest
when the wringing winds
wrench at its clinging roots
and the tempest tears at its branches
like a hawk at a summer nest.

THE ANGERED FORGE

The hammering fist of wind,
the north's keen blade of cold
shape to the greening tree
the oak's enduring mold.

It is the angered sea
caged in its ledge-rimmed home
that weaves of wave-thrown threads
a lace of silken foam.

It is the lion's claw,
the lion's tooth and need
that shape the hunted deer
to grace and speed.

Beneath my enemy
or, I, victor above,
form on anguished lips
some fearful prayer for love.

THE ROAD I MEND

Culverts, the eyes of Lucifer,
cataracted with the rooty growth of bogs
and black with the clotted blood of earth,
stare blind. After the surgery of my shovel
I can see heaven through the hollows of his eyes.

Ditches, veins of the demon,
dividing with sinews of golden gravel,
clog with corroding clay
arteries hardened by indulgence.
It is by the miracle of my hoe he lives.

Bridges, satanic towers,
the gates to high mountains and to wilderness,
rise above gardens, kingdoms
and slow rivers that could be mine
except the dust of my broom
erases the promise.

Macadam, the modern Styx,
winds more than its seven coils around the earth
carrying priests and carrying the profane
to their journey's end.
I serve the angels of light
and I serve the angels of dark
for this is the road I mend.

AFTER LOGGING

The crews have left the small orphan trees upon the hill,
struck by bewilderment, bowed every way,
weak for the rowdy winds that play rough-house
across these injured acres now.

Someone will pass and say, "The yield was good.
These saplings will stand straight within the year."
The hunter will demand his virgin wood,
leaving a trackless slashing to the deer.

Some traveler will see these thin-spaced trees
against the sky and think no more of them
nor understand why they remind him of some common thing:
a comb with coarse and broken teeth flung on the sand.

DEER AT DAWN

He kept to shadows
and tall brush,
a shadowed thing
taut and listening.
His doe
tested the hush
of empty forest
with stomping hoof.
Where was the rush
of squirrel play,
the sudden drum
of partridge hen,
the flick of bird,
the screech of jay?

The silence roared
and bugles sounded
in their blood.
They leaped and ran.

YOU NEVER SHALL ENTER

You never shall enter the soundless wood
beyond where one leaf falling builds,
hill-long, a wave of pulsed alarm
that stirs the sudden drum of partridges
or prompts the shrill cry of the blue jay's call.

You never shall enter the muted wood
beyond where snowflakes, whispering,
teach laden boughs a gentle speech;
where winds confined by frosty twigs
conspire to make the hemlocks creak.

You never shall enter the peaceful wood
beyond where eyes of sentinels
scan down the hillside where you stray.
You never shall climb by a hidden way
or an unknown path to the secret hill.

You never shall enter the silent wood
beyond where padded hooves of deer
leap down the flower beds of spring,
and snow upon the greening moss
sings down the silver sluice of streams.

13

AFTER DROUGHT

More than toad-thunder is rain on rock,
the tom-tom beating of raindrops
on the dry shingle of earth,
more than music for mountain mists dancing
over mirrors of pools,
more than drink to quench the land's thirst.

More than balm to the crusty belt
of the bellying snake is the rain
in the dry dust-bed of the grass blade
making jewels of gravel shine
bright as the eyes of a serpent
where ground swells and dank roots wade.

More than pearls to a barren coast,
more than gems for the earth's deep mines
where filtering cold sand shivers,
in the crystal bead of the raindrop
is the wisdom of all tides,
the way of all rivers.

THE GULLS

The gulls came out to meet me
even before I saw the ground swell in the sea.
Before the albatross, long following, left knowingly,
the gulls came over crying *Land !* to me.

Wise in the sea's ways, wise in the ways of ships,
they fly in the trough of the waves, their wing tips
touching the sea, and their sideslips
slide to the waves as they slide to the wake of ships.

Gulls, what do you tell me? How can I understand?
Familiar gulls, do I come to an unfamiliar land?
Do I come to the place I seek, or do I stand
always expectant with your promises, your cries of Land ?

15

HARVESTINGS

Westward, a harvesting light:
last burnished windrows rim
hills black as bays.
Great cloud-hands bind
all daybright scatterings
with lightning's wires,
clearing the path for rain.

I saw my father,
huge beside the cart,
fork double tumbles to the towering load.
One shoulder seemed to fend
the storm away,
the other leaned to gleaning tines
and reaped the hay.

INTERSECTION

Waiting for the light to change
amid arrogant looks urging swiftness,
I see him
poised on wheels touching earth lightly,
engine ready, responsive
(sails slipping the breeze).

But where can he go
dragging anchors cabled to hills
and counties, their inhabitants
ready to follow?

Even the hawk hangs in still air.
The fox barks clear.
The horn sounds in the valley.

The horn, the horns, the horns:
he presses the throttle.

MIRROR

I saw him on the shining street
with clean white hands and searching eyes.
He seemed like the strange men who passed,
save plowman's earth was on his feet.

He seemed like the strange dapper men
who danced their light steps on the street,
but I who saw him walking there
knew the wide fields of difference.

I hailed him: "Friend"—no time to lose—
"we two are of the soil," I said.
He passed me by like all the rest,
save plowman's earth was on his shoes.

RETURN

I come to these:
the shifting course of the stream,
sand silting into the old pools,
a stark light invading the secret shade.

My feet stumble on stony ruts
that were once the wagon's high road
where none but the rain goes now
singing the song of wheels.

I return to weathered barns
where only the swallows' wings
divide the spiders' curtains
to the empty mows.

Afield I come to corners
once clean for clover
where thistles glisten
above the brown brake yield.

I return to old gates.
My hand reaches out,
closes cold on the grip of the wind.
My hand shakes to the greeting.

OTHER FOLIAGE

GENESIS

(AN APRIL MORNING)

Morning without light
holds in elemental snow
all color locked in prisms
of each flake. This struggling hour,
seed of crystal fern
burn to be born
a living leaf, a flower.
Stars are flung to night.
The moon is hung;
its glacial beams
path lake and hill.
The sun is struck
for life and light.
Abundantly earth fills
with birds, fish move
in every pool.
All beasts make home.
Winds raise a primal dust.
My rib-bones ache
from lying long.
I breathe, and I awake.

CEREMONY

This day—rose:
not white bud gesturing prayer
but bloom meeting
morning's crystal hours;
pressure of beauty
pulsing at each pore,
where drink drafts of day,
beams of light;
and from whose open hands
the ant and I
bear fragrances away.

Let me burn this spectral flower
on my sight
to hold for my own hour.
Let me reason thorn, and why,
snowdrift of petals,
rust of time.
Let me remember rose
and you, and you asleep:
that though the lids be closed
your eyes may not seem ever blind, nor mine.

CLOSING CYCLE

They, knowing burn and cold,
naked stars, bold
in stillness and mystery,
gold and silver roots
holding their floods for spring,
of temptation or glory
traumaed me into the world.

Love bathed me as summer rain,
dried me on glistening stones.
I nursed honey from hidden combs.
My shirt was splendid
as the folding hills.

They gave me love and left;
left me with night and stars
and the cold mountains' care.
I wear the seasons' garments.
My unborn kin
cry softly in the wind.

SAID LOVE

I am fathomless.
I touch your hand,
a wavering delicate touch,
as lace-white foam touches
the dry sand.

I leave you
as the cooling wave
returns to the sea.
I am fathomless.
How can you understand?

I am the glint of light
on the wings of a bird
sun-caught in silver hue.
A flash. I am lost to your sight
in the tracked and trackless blue.

I am the dream,
your dream of love
when the foam-soft wave breaks home,
when the gull soars above,
the eyes perceive with joy
this visible certain grace.

You wake from the dream
when I touch your hand.
You see but the empty space.
How can you understand?

FREEDOM AND CHAINS

Soaring, I reach those currents
that could carry me toward paradise.
Then to that stillness rise
familiar sounds, voices,
earth's clamoring.
I fall, half wishing
for a tether or a broken wing.

Drifting, blind by wide staring,
I take direction of the waves.
O shipwrecked coast,
I boast my fins touch shelter
in a thousand lees:
stay my outward trip.
At last I find my pool,
a prison in a sunken ship.

Earth's citizen, she grants
me cold indifferent latitudes
of praise, frees me in deserts,
from mountains lets me gaze
until I see that home
the hills impound.
I haste to know that place again
and there by love be bound.

DESERT SCENE

Sky pressing a sea of sand
weighs down on me.
With flailing hand I sketch
protecting hills upon the curving blue:
Deer Ridge to Bailey's Cliff.
One low rise would do
from which the milk of mountains flows.
I lift my shadow up and shape a tree,
leaved to shelter me.
I pick the stones for flowers.
I have far buzzards
railing songbird spring.
With silver string I draw
the dew of cumulus
for morning shine.

Reflected blossoms
quiver in your eyes.
Enough that I dream mine.

THE DARK PRIESTESS

Brightness of your coming
leads the holy sun.
Yet part of night
is that assemblage
in your shadow's backward cast.

There you walked down morning's
rail of light with strangers
and they drowned.

There you sang hosannas
to the flesh of marble statues
and they learned a human sound.

There you threw the wreath of love
burning on the quenching sea
unrequited, unreturning.

Now the shadows leap like demons.
Priest and poet see their sermons
nailed upon the changeless tree.

Yet at zenith shadows lighten,
dark and demon cease to frighten,
for one moment visions brighten
and the sun falls all around.

WHEN SPRING IS EARLY

Snowflakes are star dust falling on her eyes,
yet waking from her dream she sees the fire
of sunlight green the crystal grass. She sees
the frost burn in the darkness of the boughs.

All bells, the icy branches chime the hour.
She hears the far-off drone of summer rise,
the rush of streams. She sees the blur of wings.
The wasp stirs on the curtain of the haze.

The slow moth wakes within the amber wood,
the willow steals the yellow of the sun,
the maple warms with red; on the hill
the orchard bears a white cloud in its limbs.

LONG DISTANCE

Our voices race midnight and morning,
hurdling the distance built
by the slopes and valleys of our lives.
Earth and air bury the impulse of our words.
Our silences tunnel the null center of noise.
Roots probe at our phrases. Worms move
secretly toward our electric speech.

Sunlight and frost fight for expansion
and compression of the stand that connects us,
itself a string singing in moonlight.
A burden of birds roosts on our sentences
while our thoughts take flight.
Our laughter runs through birdfeet;
it is clutched by claws.

Yet our voices surface to light,
closer than conversation in a room,
safer than whisperings.
There is yet time to say Hello! Goodbye!
and all that matters in between.

LAUGHTER

Laughter is lightning
and in its instant
the silent valley,
the valley of darkness,
is the garden of light,
the garden of Allah.
And in its instant
the walls of the valley fall
and the horizon
is far and afire.
A way winds outward,
a lava of moonlight,
a starry way winding
from garden unto garden.

Laughter is lightning
and the light of laughter
burns above the floods of silence,
above the tides of darkness
and the waves of night
go over and over.
The light of laughter
runs on the dark of the hills
and the leaves
answer with shining.

H$_2$O

Water, father of all tricksters,
artist of escape and legerdemain,
tumbler, dancer, runner-in-circles,
worker with easy and flowing strength,
keeper of secrets, bearer of freight,
idler lolling in ditches,
diluter, waster and destroyer,
artist of change, mirror of exactness,
stylist of diffusion, weathervane of my brow,
you have the tenderness of tears,
the fury of tempests.

With dry lips I study you
for the quicksilver of your ways.

THOUGH NOT IN ARMOR PROVED

Young and David-wise I go down
into the shadowed valley to meet my Goliath,
a stripling shepherd and unafraid
though time rattle his giant greaves,
though I hear the groan of his armor and see
his spear great as a weaver's beam.

With five small stones from the brook
and my narrow sling I go, though he raves
he will fling my flesh to the birds of the air
and yield my bones to the beasts of the fields.

Though he boasts he will win and laughs
that I carry but staves against his might
and scorn for his brassy target and foreborne shield,
his is the lie and I give him the word:
though his sword come to rest in my heart
only my hate will die
my love will live.

THE TOP

Whirl, world—
whine; wind.
I am the caught,
teased, tempted, taut child.

Spin gold, green,
splash splendor, flash,
dash gold. Twirl
round, round; run down slowly,
slowly. Top tip, tip slant,
sway, cant wide, slide.
World grown grey,
groan, grind.

I am the child.
Wind, oh wind!
Wind quickly!

known

THE SIZE OF MAN

If I am silence on a ferny hill
mine is the voice of grasses, leaves and flowers,
flames smoldering upward in the moldering wood
of sunlight tracing shadows on a stone.

If I am stone, seeming insensible but slumbering,
think that my atoms dance in planned delight.
I know the kiss of dew, the touch of rain.
I bear the hammers of enduring night.

If I am night my eyes need be the stars.
Yet I am man, so placed midway in size
between the atom and those distant suns
that all the light that makes me see is love.

36

OTHER FOLIAGE

There is an island shaped by gleaning fire,
its beaches groved with trees
whitened in flame whose curling trunks expire
as torches falling to the steaming seas.

There is an airy greening hill
where Eve stood awed in staring light
and knelt to find
a foliage like Eden's taking root:
fronds, not of substance, but fair thoughts entwined
and branches bending with remembered fruit.

TOWN REPORT

PRIVATE TRANSACTION

When Truman sold his farm to younger folks
he sought to make the deed out by himself,
he didn't hold to trite legal descriptions.
"It took me fifty years," he said, "to learn
what I had bought because it wa'n't on paper."
A certain piece of land, described To Wit:
—he smiled to think how much the law left out.
It mentioned nowhere that his hillside rose
highest above the valley for its view,
or that one half his field stood up on edge,
pinned to the mountain's steepness, so it seemed,
by two outcropping points of rusty ledge.
It never mentioned that the morning sun
most often chose to climb his pasture's line,
or that the moon, friendly and dallying,
at times played hide and seek among his pine.
He wanted to write in what he was selling:
those gnarled and twisted beech along the ridge
that never would be lumber worth the cutting.
Yet by their steadfast leaning to the weather,
for him, they held a worth beyond the telling;
that knoll of brush he had been quick to call
a waste, that ripened to wild blueberries in fall.
He'd name the alder swamp, lush and wild growing:
it took him years to learn that he had bought
a wealth in mountain springs, pure and full flowing.
Nowhere was it mentioned, when he bought
the land, of rights of animals to passage,

food and shelter; or that one rocky mound
long had been claimed by foxes as a den;
or that a falling acorn might belong
to him whose ears first heard it hit the ground.
Somewhere he'd write in the observation
that trees didn't care who they were growing for,
they'd go on meeting season after season.
He'd add one final sentence and admit
really the land could not be owned, by reason
that one life is too short quite to possess it.

THE FOX

Waiting in the dark for the fox to return
that had stolen from me so cleverly
I thought, Perhaps his mother taught him
to do these things. She must have taught him
when he could bark and when he should be still.
He was young when he learned of his shrill voice
and he and his brothers barked and played all day
on the stony hill: red foxes in the red leaves
going round and round. He could be heard there
and not be seen, but in the green open fields
he learned to slink close to the ground,
to use every cover and mound going between
the forest and the fields. He learned
to make a home in narrow ledges or underground,
a final refuge from the teeth of dogs
and the bite of winter nights. He used the trick
of stopping on a high rock or a fallen log,
looking behind him and sniffing the air
for the scent of danger. Maybe he thought, sometime,
to show his own young how to move in the night
toward a silent flock. Waiting I saw the tall stalks
part at the grasses' edge. I saw his sharp
and eager face. He crouched by an old box and looked
through the dark to the chicken yard. He glanced
about him, studying his danger, and out in the moonlight
he turned to look at the starry night.
There was flame as bright as a falling star,
and that moment fires burned fiercely in his wondering eyes.
He moved close to the ground he knew.
He did not seem young and beautiful any more
and his shaggy red fur looked mangy and worn.

IT IS EASY TO BE MISJUDGED

Because I was late with the chores,
having been to the fair, I climbed the hill
in darkness to fetch the cow and milk her,
fearing that longer delay
would dry her udder as surely
as if she had spent a day
chanking windfalls and bloating
under a sour apple tree.
She took me to be a beast of the hills
and she ran away.

My head still whirling
with whirling wheels
(I could still hear the spiels
of the barkers and see
the spinning lights and the freaks
and the flashing of everything
there on display), I walked toward her
with halter and rope
at a natural pace.
I held the lantern steady
and low at my hips
when she saw my stride change
to the lope of a wolf,
my hair grow bristly and coarse
on my face, and my teeth become
too long to be covered up
by my snarling lips.

It was not my intention
to worry her or to give chase.
I thought only to prove to her
that it was I whom she saw.
But she had her mind made up
never to let fall on her back
the weight of a he-wolf's paw.
After an hour of running
I gave up her track.

A neighbor who lives
miles away by road
brought her back to her barn
on the following day.
He had found her, he said,
entwined in the lines
the family washing hung on.
She was wearing his fanciest shirt
over one horn,
the lace of a bright pillowcase
adorned her round rear.
On seeing her barn
there was certain delight in her eyes.
You'd have thought she had really escaped
the fate of a black bear's bite
or the blade of a butcher's knife,
and she looked more than pleased with herself
that she'd saved her own life.

PASSING REMARK

Freem Jenkins had just bought a donkey.
Maybe because in certain ways it displayed
some of his own characteristics
he was unusually fond of the animal.
It wouldn't be pushed around
and it had a mind of its own.
It brayed sometimes just to hear itself.
Freem's neighbors had recognized a likeness
but the comparison had not become acute
until one of the neighbors met Freem and the donkey
walking side by side on the road one morning.
They exchanged a mild Hello
and the neighbor quickly added,
"First time I've seen you together!"

ANOTHER RANGE

If you could hear
with a special ear
the range of insect speech
oh what a din,
what a daze you'd be in;
what things that range could teach:

The crickety, crotchety, grumpy bugs
shouting their woes in one voice,
the gossipy, hoppity locust swarms
each singing the song of its choice.
What scandal, what scandal
the grapevines must handle,
what stories the fields must forget.
And the truth of the matter,
for all of the clatter,
you've heard but the least of it yet.

One old grampa spider
lays right to the cider
down at a sour-apple bar.
Some ants could be named
and their ant parents blamed,
who carried carousing too far.
They tiptoed home lightly,
for a week or more, nightly,
under an anticking star.

Two parties of mites
are demanding their rights.
Their leaders are acting like pests.
Their slogans "Begone"—
"Leave the dead limb you're on"
are taken as no idle jests.
The mites fully plan
to do what they can;
they're hurrying not in the least.
To move out, they say,
in the world, the way
is to get on the back of some beast.

The hustle one sees
at a workshop for bees
is less, to be specific,
than the queen desires
of bees she hires
(though their noise is terrific).
Yet have no fear:
if you could hear
her busy foremen shout
it would be known
that every drone
will get his combing-out.

Such acting goes on
at the aqua-salon
that boasts of the swamp's biggest band
not half the crowd's able
to get a floating leaf table,
and toadstools are spread on the land.
One termite turned green
at the sights he had seen,

but was taken, at last, by their tricks.
He told his best friends,
and the odd way it ends:
they are all moving down from the sticks.

If you would hear,
place a listening ear
to a waiting lily-phone
whose roots thread down
in the underground
to channels quite unknown.
If you would hear,
cup a listening ear
for the drum of a beetle-bone
being struck by the wings
of invisible things
in a coded monotone.
If a muffled roar
you hear, or more,
in the range of insect speech
oh what a din,
what a daze you'll be in!
What things that range will teach!

TOO EARLY AND TOO LATE

No one expected to see a stranger in Brookline
until spring roads had dried another week or more.
In fact, after the long isolation of winter
the villagers hardly were prepared to greet the spring.
Almost it seemed an affront to them
when an eager young salesman came casually
into the store for directions. "Do you know a Mr. Pratt
around here?" he asked. The storekeeper managed
a knowing "Yup" without turning his head to look
at his visitor. The salesman waited without luck
for any elaboration on his question;
"a plumber by trade," he offered. "Yup," the answer
was the same. "Well, could you direct me to where
Mr. Pratt is?" he asked, warming to the situation.
"Sure could," was the short reply. "Is it on this road?"
"Nope. Out by the cemetery." The salesman thought
he was getting somewhere at last. "How'll I find him
then?" he asked. The storekeeper coughed lightly
and said it without looking up: "Dead."

THE VISITOR

Miss Clark tried not to be noticeably different
from her country friends whom she was visiting.
She joined in their homely conversations and made
herself generally agreeable in her new surroundings.
To show her friendliness, she introduced herself
to the neighboring farmer whom she frequently met
      on the road.
He responded with, "Glad to know you." There followed
an awkward pause. Endeavoring to resume the conversation,
Miss Clark fell back upon the tell-tale truth.
"You know, I'm a spinster," she said, brightening.
The farmer looked downright puzzled at that.
Miss Clark was embarrassed. "Well, you know
what a spinster is, don't you?" she asked.
The farmer shifted nervously on his feet.
"Well sure," he said; "I've heard there's one of them
over in Rochester." Miss Clark hurried on down the road
feeling more than ever a total stranger.

HORSE STORY

One day when Pa and I was hauling wood
we came across Sam Jones and his big team
stuck almost to the hub with near a load on.
Sam sure was stuck, but gosh it didn't seem
he'd be so willing to give up and ask for help.
Pa didn't hesitate; he saw the chance
to make a pleasant story he could tell.
"Gosh, Sam," he said, "you've seen my horses prance,
you've seen 'em draw and know the loads we haul.
I dare you let me hitch my team on there
and show you what a mated pair can do."
Pa knowing Sam wa'n't one to take a dare.

A bit excited like, Pa hitched 'em on.
You should have seen the spirit that they showed,
the way they danced and looked behind 'em like.
You'd know they sensed it wa'n't the usual load.
Pa knew every trick that starts a team:
the Gee and Haw—the Woops, come here!—Let's go!
the sidewise draw and then the steady pull,
the seesaw back and then the sudden Whoa!
I saw Pa tighten on the reins a bit.
The way he looked I knew that he was ready.
"Come here!" he called. And how those horses pulled.
You never saw two horses quite so steady.
You know—arched necks, low stance, their feet out wide,
weight throwed ahead, and even on the draw.

You'd know to see the way their heads were held
they'd pull more'n any team you ever saw.
They came up easy till the tugs were tight.
Well, you should've been there. Then I guess you wouldn't
been s'prised to hear how far they pulled that load:
they just couldn't budge it and I knew they couldn't.

LANDMARK

Clem Hawkins finally came back to town.
He'd been away near twenty years,
and came a-driving back about midspring
at just about the time of year he'd left.
Still, things looked pretty puzzling to old Clem;
you know how twenty years will change a place.
He couldn't see a natural-looking thing—
that it, until one mudhole stretched in view.
He found some cars were stuck there in the mud.
Clem knew how he could help, so he got out.
"Now pull into those ruts right there," he said,
"and drive straight through, and you'll make out just fine,
'cause they're the ones I took when I left town."
Then Clem looked fondly at the scene and said,
"You know, there's some things that just never change.
It does seem good to be back home again."

REMINISCENCE

Levi Sutton had had quite a career.
He never lost much sleep over it though,
not as a rule; but this night was different.
Maybe he'd been thinking of his younger days
and trying some of his capers all over.
He didn't know himself just where he was;
the usual place, he thought. He reached out
and sure enough he felt the iron bars.
No such jail would hold old Levi Sutton:
he let both feet do some kicking then.
A bit surprised to feel how the bars bent,
he stuck his head through and tried to get out.
But somebody was coming with a light.
He couldn't get his head back, so he stayed there.
It was Ma Sutton, and she was feeling cross.
"Levi," she yelled and shook him hard,
"wake up and get your head out of that bedstead;
if you have any more of these nightmares
you can take your duds and sleep in the barn."

SPRING SONG

Knee deep, knee deep!
Knee deep, knee deep!
The cow is out.
The peepers peep.

Knee deep, knee deep!
The swamp is wide.
The pasture's on
the other side.

Knee deep, knee deep!
But some deceive.
A boy could wade,
but don't believe.

She's over there;
the cow is found.
Knee deep, knee deep!
Better go round.

Better go round!
Better go round!
Better go round!
Echoes the sound.

She's over there.
The voices now:
Dan Dow, Dan Dow
here is your cow.

Dan Dow, your cow.
She's there—one leap.
Better go round!
Knee deep, knee deep!

CROW CONVENTION

Talk, talk, talk, colder tomorrow;
like as not frost, black as a feather.
Shock, shock, shock, piled in the cornfield.
There is your warning of used-up weather.

Stalk, stalk, stalk, goldenrod waving;
gentians are bright October blue.
Walk, walk, walk, on the stubble of harvest.
Wings to the south, summer is through.

Bah, bah, bah, sheep on the short feed
nibbled close as a stone to the ground.
Ah, ah, ah, the moon is brighter;
mornings are later in getting around.

Haw, haw, haw, leave the fields lonely;
let scarecrows stand in gardens of snow.
Caw, caw, caw, sun and the southland:
warn all the valley tomorrow we go.

THE ABSENT SMITH

There was a blacksmith in a town I know,
at least there was until a while ago,
who some folks say the devil took for hire
to teach him what he knew about a fire.

That he could draw a temper it was true.
He knew his trade and other business too,
one reason that his shop was always filled
before he left, or died, or yet was killed.

The shop is empty now. The tools are there
as bright as though they were in constant wear.
Though no one opens up the long-locked door
some say the coal runs low—and then there's more.

Neighbors arguing about his fate
who have no reason to exaggerate
have sworn they heard his anvil being struck,
which gives small hope to what has been his luck.

I've heard they saw within his shop a light
made by his blazing forge one stormy night.
One shadow held another with great pains.
Above the roar they heard the clank of chains.

Some say he's drawing out the hardened souls
who lost their temper in the devil's coals.
Some say he just left town and not this life.
Some say he fell for a young farmer's wife.

PERL'S WALK

There are no journeys left
for an old man, dim of sight
and deaf, no road better
than the grassy road to town.
He will walk that path
until his last,
carrying the brown sack
for his simple needs.
Tomorrow he will return
asking for the unexpected letter.

How the hill changes.
Truman is dead,
Rogerses moved away,
the Yeaws not home.
There are no neighbors
left along that road;
no place inviting him
to stop and lean his back
against a dooryard gate
to rest and talk.
The hill to town is steeper now,
and it is a longer walk.

THE LOGGER'S SUNDAY HOME

He asked her to be careful on this day.
One pail of water was enough to bring.
"You'll hurt yourself by hurrying," he'd say,
"with two full brimming buckets from the spring."

Kindly he'd help her through the narrow door.
He'd scoop one clear, cool dipperful to drink,
making a little show of draining it
that not one crystal bead waste in the sink.

Feeling her need for him in his own way
he'd check to see if all the wood was burned
that kept the family warm on winter nights
from heaps of icy slabs, as she had learned.

This day, for once, he asked about the saw.
He filed and set the teeth the best he could,
letting her try it that it draw across
the way she liked it best for frozen wood.

For such a day he did not ask to sit
and talk, with playing children all about.
The early evening lamp was scarcely lit;
the beds were made and the dim light put out.

NO NEW THING

She needed no new thing
they said, being so old.
She'd kept on her thin shelf the cloak
for this strange cold.

She needed no new words,
no news to dread.
Between the covers of her days
all had been said.

In life she asked for so few things
for happiness.
They all stood dumb to learn in death
she asked not less.

MILLHAND

The big saw asked nor gave
no quarter in its task.
Eventually one careless hand
fell with the frozen slabs,
scorned in the whining mill.
Like a dropped glove
he brought it back
from the tainted sawdust,
held it to his numbed wrist again,
fitting it perfectly, before he fainted.

An iron hand can hold
a pipe, a shovel, carry a pail.
An iron hook hardly can fail
at anything
an unskilled hand can do.
Better than part of him
it knows no insult
of rude act or weather.
He can drive spikes
with his fingers.

Metal, it can not feel
the world's rejection,
the dog's recoil when
cold and common steel strokes its hair.

His fortune, a twisted iron
in a tattered sleeve,
is not more incongruous
than his final inheritance:
an old sleigh horse
and a wagon for winter.

GIB'S BARN

Time wrought the silver finish of Gib's barn.
The weather working always at the wood's deep grain:
the kiln-sun drawing the last resin of the boards,
the dry fibers drinking only the varnish of rain.

Some loved it for its age and lonely place,
a farm left backward by the main highways.
Birds loved it for its eaves and pigeons' cote
and for its empty scaffold on foul days.

Its wood was fit for violins and sounding pins.
It was itself a silent instrument at last.
The huge beams, taut, between the floor and roof
trembled inaudibly to echoes of its past.

Lying now a puzzle of bent beams,
at times some loose board creaks as though its stable door
was opened, and one hears pitchforks rasp the wood
and horses stomping on the thick-planked floor.

OLD GAMBLER'S TALE

I told him the fort was burned
but he said as he turned
a card: "We'll finish the game."
I said: "They're at Bunker Hill."
He motioned that I be still.
"Play," he said. "That's why I came."

"We're losing at Gettysburg."
He dealt without saying a word.
He had his own battle with me.
"They're shelling Paris," I said,
as he laid down one of the red,
"they'll drive right through to the sea."

"They've struck in the islands," I gasped.
I started to rise as he grasped
my arm in a painful way.
"We'll need more force in the east."
It disturbed him not in the least.
"You'll stay," he said, "and you'll play."

I saw he was cheating me then.
As he shifted an ace for a ten
I put a long knife to his head.
"Fear," I called him by name,
"this is the end of the game.
They're needing me now," I said.

LATE TO THE TOWN

Because the rack o' bones he drove
paced nearer to his final home,
because fate set him so alone,
old Milo reined his horse about
for one more journey to the town.
He chuckled that with wit he still
could cheat fate with his stubborn will.
The landscape changed beneath his wheels.

In Higley's lane the walls were down
that kept the pasture from the road.
A thoroughfare ran through the fields
Higley until his last had mowed.
His lane that once showed hoof-worn wear
was closed beyond his maple hill,
and Higley's rusting plow still slumped
in one unfinished furrow there.

The friendly covered bridge was gone
he long had loved as one thing left
that linked the present with the past;
a bridge that reached from age to youth.
Distraught, he braced himself to cross
the river's modern concrete span
where guardrails in the moonlight shone
like trim white rows of burial stones.

He saw the town's bright lights ahead.
He thought the roistering boys were back;

he shouted and he waved his cane,
he hurried toward the lively spot.
The lights were moonlight on each pane
of the street's huge and empty church.
The glowing windows turned to black.
He bowed his head in dourful thought.

He sought the road's cool watering trough.
He stopped beside an arid space
where culverts drank from underground.
He thirsted and he tried to think
how many times, how many trips
this spot had been a saving place.
A fire of anger rose in him
and parched the desert of his lips.

He thought he heard the bellows roar
where late the blacksmith kept his shop.
He stopped beside the darkened door.
He heard the heaving of his horse.
The bright enameled walls bore out
the certain meaning of it all,
told in the warring signs above
that urged the motorist to stop.

"Enough of this rude change of things;
Old Schuyler, take me home!" he cried.
He whipped Old Schuyler with the reins;
he braced his body for the ride.
"Faster!" he urged, unquestioning.
His wheels were stars with fiery rims;
he nodded to their answerings.
He slept, and sleeping he had wings.

WEATHER CHANGE

BIRDS IN THREE MOODS

I

A sunflower sun gazes
over the gate of the hills.
Morning wakes with petaled ease.
A giant strides the footprint fields.
I am he who stoops
to walk beneath the song-filled trees.

II

I bow to the size of man
at sun-stopped noon and see
enchantment level to reality.
My journey is toward the night.
Songbirds fight for seeds
on the weedy lawn.

III

The shadows of their wings
are vulture size. The road is long.
Moon-bald and strange are all the birds I know.
A heaviness in me draws as though
on a branch of my heart
they fastened with eagle claws.

WEATHER CHANGE

Sapphire stars
of treasure-laden night,
I drop you coin by coin,
spendthrift, on daylight's street.

Now before the great
grey bank of evening
I stand in poverty.
O passers-by,
lend me the currency of smiles.

NOW ARE THE HILLS ON FIRE

Driven by the quickening autumn blaze
the wolf-wind runs his burning timber trails
stirring so soon a frozen dust like ash.
The haze, the smoke of frost at every tree
signal the glow of foliage fires below.

Circling his hill, the homing hawk
screeches above the flames
that reach the tinders of his nest.
Small birds have flown. Lush green has grown
to red that mocks the sunset west.

Safe in fir cathedrals kneel the wise,
resting their eyes on somber moss and ferns.
Such conflagration leaps now through the wood
only hope calms the rabbit-jumping blood.

NEW SNOW

The village, burdened with the weight of storm,
labors in the clock-tick of the hours.
Midnight lanterns burn toward dawn.
Diesels adjust their instruments; engines moan
as snowplows lift the night upon their wings.
Morning will find the new snow resting here.
The busy homes will turn to usual things,
the meals, the chores; yet in every house
low voices now and knowing smiles
and tiptoe steps that would not wake a child.

SALT-LICK PASTURES

My graceful deer
leap from the thicket of combers
electric with old fear of open space.
They run on the sea-sloped meadow.
The dry sand barks at their heels.

They cannot feed in salt-lick pastures;
they must find the hemlock cover,
the high stand of oak.
                  I hear them again, rested,
working the forest for acorns.
Leaves pile about them like broken waves.

Their low rustling is the returning
of the sea.

TIDE

Rise foam and fall. Sea
turn in a growing agony.
Will it soothe to shatter
the glass of your tortured calm
on the headland reef?

Splay foam and vend
your pressed and gathered grief
to the weathered shore.
Your mood is his
who studies your caged despair
while the welling tide floods in.

GRAND CANYON

Birds dive, they rise again.
I stand with leaden feet.
I clutch the crevice-anchored roots.
I feel an ice-cave chill
the glacier left.
I seek the sureness of the canyon floor
and there
I gaze into the crater
of a flower.

TO BE AWARE

Nobody's dog at the door
hinders my going.
He tests me with sad eyes
for an offering.
He is mine, mine forever,
would I recognize his gaze,
would I say "Dog, come in"
or speak his name.

THE CONSTANT LURE

Rainbows are hidden
under the dark rocks
and hooks of sunlight play
for the hungry fishes' eyes.

There is the flash of bubbles'
silver spoons; and thin
each shadow line and rod
of nimble cherry lies.

Slowly the hours tighten
a net of shadows
drawing the frightened
fish to shore.

Rainbows scatter into arcs
of lightning freed
in the thundering crash,
the swift stream's roar.

ARABESQUE

Through mist the leafy cones
of maples are domes
of mosques. The spruce are spires.
Rows of field-brought vegetables
make this the market place.

Indolent merchants
spread their leaf-wrought tapestries
upon the stones. A gifted one
plays his strange music in the square
on pipes he fashions there
of vines and whistlewood.
Before him like a cobra sways
the yellowing ivy at the grasses' edge.
Poplars, wealthy sahibs
lordly dressed, drop
their coin of golden leaves
to urchin undertrees.

This jostling market crowd
has all the bleach and blend
of colors at a summer's end.
Each priestly pine offers a murmured prayer,
and everywhere with fitful fingers
work the forty thieves of wind.

AS OF NOW

We buried the horses,
closed the mow,
carried our crutches waiting.
Grass grew high
about the barn and house.
Trees bore bitten apples.
Junipers sprung in pastures.
Milkweed threw windward
its robust seed.
Paintbrush reddened the field.
The barn's bay gaped unfilled.

I ran out into the sunlight,
my scythe whetted with fire,
and I tired
on the first tier of the hill.

The saved daisies gestured joy,
the steeplebush praise.
Moving back from brake,
from encroaching pine
I walked the swath-line home,
a fierce heat upon my hands and brow
a chill advancing along my spine.

THE POET

On my Olympus
by fate I was assigned
with working gods.
One god was blind.

He would make poems
in the vineyard shade
and taste the ripened grapes.
He would not spade.

I did his share
until my fingers bled
pruning the extra vines.
I wished him dead.

I reasoned then
that he would never trim
his keeping's worth alone.
I murdered him.

He has revenge.
To my surprise
a blindness falls on me
who touched his dying eyes.

PROPHECY

I shall be legend
among the unnumbered:
a rib of earth
in shifting sand,
garnet in crumbling ledge
indifferent to weather,
or hollow of hollows
a clay saucer for water,
saltless among salt waves,
white in grey ashes,
a strange breath left
in the wind's wake.

I hear the winds say,
playing a winnowing game,
"This dust is not the same."
I shall be legend.

SUN DOWN

Sing the sun down
into the west of dreams,
to lost chances, to deeds
undone, to the juncture of roads
where the traveler stands
already knowing where one road leads.

Chant the sun down
into that tide of darkness
unfathomed by compass or chart
where all distractions are lost
and the eyes see clearly only
that which is written upon the heart.

Dance the sun down
under the rim of the world
where time stands meaningless.
Only such darkness has space
narrowed to the width of two hands
on the breadth of a face.

THAT PATH JOY GOES

I will forge bells
for leaden days.
I will form dust
into a diamond wreath,
in storm see
jeweled light
move like a scythe
through ripened grain,
in drouth find rain
gushing from smitten stone.
After night's watch,
in morning glow,
almost, almost I know
that path joy goes.

Dear Beth,

Everyday is valentine
the times I spend with
you, o the times I'm
thinking about you
Is all the times I
miss you when you're
not there